I Know Something
You Don't Know!

Which animal runs fastest?

The cheetah is the fastest-running animal. A cheetah can run
at speeds of more than 75 miles per hour. That's about three
times faster than the fastest human in the world.

Brigitte Raab · Manuela Olten

I Know Something You Don't Know!

FINISH

NorthSouth
New York / London

"My uncle's favorite cow gives so much milk, we could open a milk bar!" said Tessa.

Could that be true? Julian visited Tessa's uncle, and his favorite cow really did make a lot of milk.

Tessa was right.

A single cow can give 30 liters of milk a day. That's about 32 quarts, or 8 gallons.

But a cow only gives that much milk for a few months after she has had a calf.

"My mom saw a bird going faster than our car!" said Bruno.

"That we've got to see!" Melissa and Justin
sat down to watch for a fast-flying bird,
but not a single bird sped past during
their entire picnic. They decided to ask
Melissa's Aunt Susan, the ornithologist.
An ornithologist is a bird scientist.

Bruno was right.

When hunting, a
falcon can reach
a speed of more
than 125 miles per
hour. That's twice
as fast as the
speed limit on
many highways.

Falcons dive down
from the sky to
grab their prey—
mostly small birds.

"When I blow on a dandelion, some of the seeds fly more than a mile!" said Matilda.

"Let's give it a try!" cried Ben and Greg, but their dandelion fuzz only flew as far as the sandbox. Later, though, when they weren't looking, the wind carried the dandelion fuzz on.

Matilda was right.

Dandelion seeds
hang on small
"parachutes."
When the wind
catches them,
they can fly for
a very long way.

That's why
dandelions grow
all over the place.

"The parrot in the zoo is older than my grandpa," said Eric.

Fred wanted to know if that could be true, so he asked the bird keeper at the zoo.

Eric was right.

Parrots can get
to be as old
as people.

Some parrots can
live more than sixty
years. Large parrots,
such as macaws
and cockatoos, can
live for seventy or
eighty years.

Polly 1943–2007

"The ants in our garden are stronger than weight lifters!" said Jason.

Could that be true? Lewis and Gus decided to explore. They discovered some ants carrying twigs much bigger than the ants themselves.

Jason was right.

Ants can carry things that are ten times heavier than they are.

Not even the best weight lifter can match that. If he could, he'd be able to lift a car and carry it around.

"A butterfly in my yard can smell a butterfly in my grandma's yard in the next town!" said Finn.

Amy didn't believe it. Amy couldn't
smell her grandma's perfume, and
her grandma lived next door.

Finn was right.

Some butterflies can smell much better than we can, and butterflies don't even have noses! They use their wings to smell things.

A male butterfly can smell a female butterfly several miles away.

"My dad's elephant is the heaviest animal in the world," said Conrad.

Really? Conrad's dad was in charge of the circus, so he should know, but Francie wasn't too sure. She had a book about animals, which she read to the others.

Conrad was wrong.

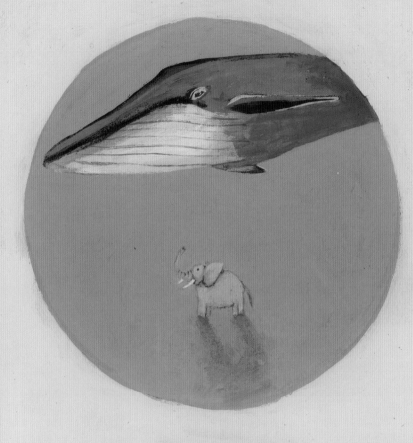

Blue whales are
heavier than elephants.
Much, much heavier.

A blue whale
weighs about
thirty times more
than an elephant.

First published in the United States, Great Britain, Canada, Australia, and New Zealand in 2010
by North-South Books Inc., an imprint of NordSüd Verlag AG, CH-8005 Zürich, Switzerland.
Distributed in the United States by North-South Books Inc., New York 10001.

Library of Congress Cataloging-in-Publication Data is available.
ISBN: 978-0-7358-2303-7 (trade edition)
Printed in China by Toppan Leefung Packaging & Printing
(Dongguan) Co., Ltd., Dongguan, P.R.C., April 2010
1   3   5   7   9 • 10   8   6   4   2

www.northsouth.com